D0885886

FROM
HOOD TO
GOOD

DWIGHT ALLEN

authorHOUSE®

AuthorHouse™
1663 Liberty Drive
Bloomington, IN 47403
www.authorhouse.com
Phone: 1 (800) 839-8640

Published by AuthorHouse 06/01/2016

ISBN: 978-1-5246-1151-4 (sc)
ISBN: 978-1-5246-1150-7 (hc)
ISBN: 978-1-5246-1149-1 (e)

Library of Congress Control Number: 2016908904

Print information available on the last page.

Contents

Certified Thug

What is a certified thug? Or what is a real man? These are questions people think about

when growing up in cities across America: Newark, Chicago, Detroit, LA,

DC, Miami, Atlanta, Dallas, Houston, Richmond, Norfolk City, Raleigh, Charlotte,

Memphis, New Orleans, Harlem, Brooklyn, Queens, Long Island, New York City,

Philadelphia, Cleveland, etc.

A thug of the streets, no matter where in the world, will have a heart, tattoos,

leadership qualities, and intensity. Not all thugs are illiterate in the same way. There is a

variety of types: gang, fraternity, street, intellectuals, and the most well known: corporate thugs.

There are guys that are suspected of being thugs; but a real man takes responsibility

for his actions and supports and protects his family. Thug thinking might be appropriate at

times when people disrespect you as a man, but do not thug it out to the point where you are constantly in and out of jail.

Remember, your street credits should be how much of a positive impact you

have in building your community and not destroying your community,

brick by brick.

A certified thug is one who knows when to use his thug card and when not to

use his thug card. He understands when he is too old to hang in the streets.

At this point, it's time for a change, and that change is to do something constructively

powerful for your family, such as start your own business or work diligently in the

workforce.

The Race Against the Clock

There is a race against time in the Black community. Slave thinking is over.

Moreover, we do not have to be in jail, in shackles and chains. Black people, wake up

and realize that you are powerful. We have a president who won in 2008 and 2012,

and we are continuing to build our families and communities, and to attain education. Staying in and

out of jail is not the answer; changing our thinking is our solution. And the white man is not

our problem; perhaps sometimes we can be our own worst enemy.

Do not fool yourself, thinking that negative thinking will keep you ahead; perhaps

you reap what you sow. When someone becomes incarcerated in the same way, that

person's family does that time as well, and this becomes very stressful to parents,

aunts, uncles, and siblings. Keep track of your time with work, school, and less street

activity. Our youths need truth, Black history, confidence, and education.

3

Young men, use the clock in your favor and not against you. Time is valuable.

Time should not be wasted with negative acts. Successful thinking will

keep you out of trouble.

Hoochie Mama

Some guys love a *hoochie mama*. However, some women are

conservative; hence, a lot of men in the ghetto prefer a ghetto fabulous vixen boo.

Some *hoochie mamas* are so damn fine, sweet, thick, thin, and juicy that

to the hood they are irresistible.

Hoochie mamas dance in the club; indeed, hoochie mamas dance

in the bar, and by all means hoochie mamas dance on the block. Drama all day

and all night, out of sight, so comical, they are the talk of the party.

It does not matter if you are ghetto at this rate. There is no need for

anyone to hate, because the hood has her back: down South hoochie mama,

up top hoochie mama, Midwest hoochie mama, and West Coast hoochie

mama. Moreover, this is what gets the thugs excited, delighted, and always in the

mood to make that hoochie mama, always wanting to stay in the game and keep things

poppin', cracking, and on point.

Urban Dime Diva

Every man in the hood recognizes an *urban dime diva* because

real women are not a dime or a dozen. This lady holds her man and family

down: cooks, clean, nurtures, and keeps a strong presence wherever she travels.

I love a woman who takes care of herself, loves herself, and by all means is

God-fearing. There are five-star chicks in the hood, and there are also women that

are ghetto and professional at the same time. Moreover, just because you are from

an urban area does not mean you can't be successful.

There are many types of women in cities across America: business,

corporate, religious, strippers, entertainers, models, video vixens, at-home

mothers, educators, lovers, and heart breakers.

Lastly, respect and support your urban dime diva, because she is real and will

appreciate your presence. It takes a real man to appreciate a good woman.

Street Smart

In the hood, it is an asset to be street smart in the way that you know

who your true friends are, how to earn money legally, how to take initiative, lead, be

a man, and handle your responsibilities at home.

No matter how mentally or physically tough, a man from the streets must be the

following: he must understand that knowledge, wisdom, common sense,

and respect are his best friends.

When you break the law, perhaps you are falling in the hands of the law in the same

way. We as men and women in cities must empower, build, unite, and keep our

communities strong.

Every urban area needs every man to stand up, protect, pray for his families, and make

our people of color stronger and more prepared for tomorrow. Surrounding the intelligence of

ambition, money, power, and respect, being street smart is being business smart. Furthermore, improve your potential, think highly of yourself, and never think that you can't be successful.

Success is granted to the hood as long as you are willing to live on point and not

get caught in the system.

Our Children Matter in All Cities

Every year is a new generation. And, yes, growing up poor is a struggle,

and it seems impossible to handle. No matter what, our children

must never quit. Our children are our future.

All adults—parents, teachers, and mentors—play a very important role in our

children's lives. We as a community must embrace our children's dreams and

constantly support their goals and bright objectives as well.

If we give a child 10 percent of our time, it can make a powerful impact on his or her

education and dynamic journey. When we are conscious and consistent,

we can strive to shape

their bright minds. As a result, our children will become powerful leaders and innovators

for our future. We must never let our children forget our African-American

history. Yes, what occurred yesterday can make a positive impact on our

opportunities tomorrow.

Love our urban kids, support our urban kids, teach our urban kids, enlighten

our urban kids.

Lastly, remember it is always about giving

our children great opportunities. And yes, at all times, our children really do

matter.

Hustle Man, Hustle Woman

Every hood has a hustle man: a vendor of car services, loose cigarettes, fake

bus cards—a "can you spare a dollar?" or "can I get a quarter sir, please?" man.

It takes the same amount of time to hustle as to work two jobs trying to make ends

meet as well as provide for your family.

True indeed, there are people in the hood that do want a nice car,

home, and wardrobe as well as the ability to vacation and travel.

Yes, there are hustle men and hustle women doing hair at home,

baby-sitting, dating, selling dinners, doing transportation, etc.

Both men and women hustle to survive because of today's inflation

and at times the unemployment factor. In the hood, only the strong survive;

instinct has been passed down through many generations.

People of color always have managed to survive any type of

recession; moreover, we hustle until we ball, and we never quit until we

have met our goals and objectives.

A hustle is an attitude; a hustle is also making rent and utilities.

And a rent party is frequent in the hood in order to pay all the bills:

rent, car note, bus card, phone, and cable.

Lastly, never knock a hustle, because in

urban areas, this is how people survive. Both men

and women hustle smart as well as hard.

Material vs. Matter

Matter can't be created or destroyed. In cities,

what matters is your priorities, because you must pay your bills

first and then travel without hesitation. Materialism and excitement

will always follow. What matters is that you take care of family

and reward yourself well when the time is appropriate.

Pray for Wisdom, Guidance, and Understanding

Material is not to be worshipped but appreciated.

Matter is what God provides, and we all should be grateful

for the blessings that God gives us. Most importantly, stay focused

and stay away from negative people who do not strive for excellence,

because you are a child of God.

Hood Struggle

Every day in any city in America can be a struggle; it's a battle

and a war on the streets: crime, haters, violence, prostitution, and opposition.

What is your position? Furthermore, what is your strategy?

And what is your exit strategy? Just because you are from the hood

does not mean you have to embrace low self-esteem or be ashamed of your city.

Every city has a history that we must research to understand

why it has its struggles. Even though this may be true, we all must have a

plan of action in place: work diligently, travel, reward yourself, build your family,

build your community, and give 100 percent to everything you do.

When you acquire education, your struggle can turn into luxurious living;

in fact, many professions require a degree or certification.

Or you may decide to become an entrepreneur. As proof of instance, at this point,

you can become ambitious and beat all odds of "a hood struggle."

Keep a high self-esteem, believe in yourself, and think *powerful*.

When you write your plan of action, execute it without a debate;

you are on the road to success, moving forward to excellence,

greatness, and unstoppable excitement.

Urban Unity

The key to any man or woman becoming successful is to have unification

within your friendships, marriage, or family. We all strive for plenty of finances,

and we combine our resources and education to build

a successful business, goal, objective, or even dynasty.

Unity, furthermore, is everyone coming together in one accord, in harmony,

thinking on the same page. People of color can't have unity

without being friendly, having family, or being positive about their outlook on life.

There is no room for doubt in your path to success. People of color,

at this point we must stand up and encourage our neighbors when they are down.

Pray for unity, church, family, friends, strength, improvement,

and most important, for those that are less fortunate in cities.

A positive comments, smile, laugh, or gesture, can cheer someone up.

There is no room for division in unity. Think quality, think *big*, think *outstanding*, and most importantly, take others into consideration. My country is the

United States of America; unity is our state of mind.

Remember there are positive initiatives in your city that you can be a part of.

Perhaps this step is a powerful step.

Lastly, build your community block by block, and your unity will stay strong

in your city.

No Chains on Your Brains

We are of all ages, men of color and women of color;

nevertheless, we must never be brainwashed that

we can't achieve success.

Our people are in fact the first people on the planet,

so every race comes from us. The Black gene

is the most dominant gene on the planet.

Black people! There should be no chains on your thinking, your

speaking, your wrists, ankles, or brains. On the contrary, confidence is

the key to breaking the chains off my people—yes, breaking the chains

and elevating our thinking.

Also, Black people, we must move forward with power,

prayer, unity, and perseverance. Be a rocket in your community

and uplift your people, because our people are well rounded:

politicians, military leaders, doctors, lawyers, entrepreneurs, inventors,

and, yes, a president and first lady in the White House.

Devote your life to excellence, structure, morals, and values, and to outdoing your progress month by month. We must increase our

energy directed toward our youths and build a better tomorrow.

Think *amazing, powerful, outstanding*, and you will

break the chains.

Lastly, exemplifying greatness,

intelligence, and motivational strength will make people of color and our

nation stronger.

Black History

Our history—yes, Black history—is a powerful history: Mr. Barak H. Obama, first Black president; Mrs. Michelle Obama, first Black

First Lady; Dr. Mary McCloud Bethune, educator, teacher; Dr. Martin

Luther King Jr., nonviolent advocate for equality for people of color;

the Honorable Thurgood Marshall, Supreme Court Justice; Rev. Jesse

Jackson, Rainbow Coalition; Rev. Al Sharpton, National Action Network;

and many more legends, present and past.

I would like to give a shout-out to all Land Grant institutions as well

in addition to private and public historically Black colleges and universities

all over the United States. I also acknowledge all Black college presidents and all

professors, teachers, counselors, and administrators that work with

great effort for all students at all levels of education.

I can't forget all parents, mentors, coaches, band directors, and music

teachers. We must keep Black history known, all inventors and Black historians, present, past, and future, remembered every month so our youth can be empowered and

become powerful leaders.

Lastly, before there was any history, there was and still is

Black history."

Education Defeats Poverty

Acquire a high-quality education, trade, or career that has growth and financial

potential to keep you and your family away from poverty. It is sad to say that today

in America, people in many parts of our country live in poverty.

Consequently, parents, make sure that your children

learn responsibility and work in their teen years; this teaches our youth great

responsibility at a young age. Poverty can't exist when people unite,

working together as communities, churches, and schools to help each other when help is

needed.

Choosing jobs that have health benefits, fair wages, and pay increases

keeps a man or woman ahead of the game: prosperous and motivated to succeed.

Excel and fight against poverty. Save your money, shop smart, eat right, exercise, pray,

and make your family work together to build a pleasing tomorrow.

Remember, what you do right today will help you succeed tomorrow. Always be grateful

for what you have, and be patient for what God has for you. Stay blessed and

keep God first.

I Will *Think* to That!

In urban areas, it seems like there is a liquor store almost everywhere; however, in the suburbs, liquor is purchased at the grocery stores and supermarkets. In the hood, winos, junkies, and alchis hang around the liquor stores to beg for change. Do not get me wrong; I know that there are alcoholics in the hood and also in suburban America.

Be a prolific thinker, and build your body as well as your family. Drink on occasions to celebrate. A red or white wine is healthy, as acknowledged by any doctor. Your liver is necessary to survive. Alcohol is a drug, and heavy depressants set people of color four hundred years back.

Encourage your friends, family, and loved ones to think, eat, and drink healthfully and responsibility. Put on your thinking caps, and drop the bottles.

Drink water and juice. Exercise your mind and body, folks. I will *think* to that!

Pay Back and Pay Black

Black people need to build lines of credit by paying all bills on time

as much as possible. Charge what you need, and buy when it is necessary.

We all love to travel, so pay your bills on time so that every four to five months

you can plan a nice relaxing vacation. As you pay your bills, you can start paying on

your vacation.

Airlines allow you to pay one-way tickets separately.

At times this method is a cheaper strategy.

Most companies offer

overtime. Utilize that overtime to pay your bills on time. Move

toward buying all your items on sale to save money all year around.

Remember, the more you save on food, clothing, and other items,

the more money in your pockets and less stress in your home.

Lastly, pay yourself first, and always have room to mobilize your family.

Ghetto Girl

Ghetto girl, ghetto girl, goes to the store
with pj's on and a scarf, no doubt.

When she is dressed up, in the same way she
looks so damn good. Ghetto girl has

an attitude as a self-defense against those guys
who may try to be disrespectful

toward her sisterhood. Ghetto girl will fight
you, cuss you out, if you even think

about being ratchet toward her or her kids.

Some ghetto girls are well educated and extremely street smart;

subsequently, don't sleep on them. Some ghetto
girls are gold diggers, strippers,

baby mamas, or just average descent women
who want better for their family

and themselves. Just because a young lady
comes from the ghetto does not mean

that she can't achieve success.

The Source of Achievement Is Yours

No matter what hood or city you are, the source of achievement

is you. We all know that most suburban schools have more resources than

urban schools; however, it is imperative that children in urban schools achieve

their dreams, goals, and objectives.

It is a fact that if you touch greatness, feel powerful, speak dynamically,

walk confidently, and think wisely, the source of achievement is yours.

People of color, stand up. Think clear. Be liquor- and drug-free, and move with confidence.

Build your neighborhoods with love.

What happened to the *neighborhood* communication? A lot of hood and no

neighbor? I do not think so! Parents, friends, family, and community,

keep your neighbors safe by getting to know them, looking out for each other. And,

most importantly, pray for your neighbors. Take success each day and keep ambition each day; maintain confidence in every way. No matter what,

the source of achievement is always yours.

Take success each day and keep ambition each day. Maintain confidence

in every way. No matter what, the source of achievement is always yours.

Child Support

Child support, child support, coming for that check. Oh my goodness, what happened

to my paycheck?

Men, believe me, some women get with men so that they can have

a child-support check and go party with their girlfriends. Men, support your kids, and

make sure you keep a job, because any judge in family court will expect those payments

as soon as possible.

Women sometimes say they are on birth control or their tubes are tied, burned, or clipped.

Men, do not fall for the drama. In addition, men should always use protection; condoms

are a must. Some women work while others stay on public assistance. Men must

choose women that are ambitious and ladies that will achieve for themselves and their family

and will not go around *trapping* men for child support checks.

Child support can be in reverse when the woman makes more money than the man.

In the same way, you have gold digging men who seek to lay up with highly ambitious women,

to get them pregnant and then try to take the child away through custody court,

truly or falsely proving that the mother is unfit. Folks, each state's laws vary

when it comes to child support. Yet no matter what, the child will lose when

the parents are fighting, bickering, backbiting, and not finding a future for

their child or children.

Remember, parents, to take care of your family and handle your business

appropriately.

Lastly, keep your children safe and happy in a healthy environment.

Banging Sex

There's nothing like banging sex, the type of sex to make you

flex or go in and say, "Ho baby, just put it in."
Foreplay, nonstop on top, makes

it rock. Yes, oral pleasure is great for men and women.

Don't tease me or make me call out your
name in ecstasy. Boo, it's no shame.

You can't half in making love, and you got to
rock her top, bottom, side, and middle.

Taste those juices as they flow with ease; in
addition, give a hot passionate kisses, and

passion marks the spot. Remember, keep it
hot and sweet and always make love

when you are in *heat*.

He's in Love with a Hoe?

He's in love with a hoe? Her loving is so damn good

that when he is with her, perhaps he just can't say no.

She is so irresistible, sexy, and a great catch.

Her attitude is so sassy, sensual, and she will throw shade if she

does not get her way.

That hoe loves to be spoiled, and she takes and never

gives.

Subsequently, your lady must have your back, and you

should not want a *gold digger*.

Remember, you can't ever possibly think that you will

turn a hoe into a housewife.

Hella Ass

Oh no! That girl got hella ass.

When she walks down the street, you know she's a lady,

and when she's in public, guys' heads turn and
they say, "Damn, she have hella ass."

This lady has curves you would not believe; perhaps she is *bodacious,*

sweet, plump, juicy, and *irresistible.* She can be any sister that you have

seen before.
When you look at that booty, you just want
to look at it more and more.

If your lady has *hella ass,* watch out! You will enjoy those juicy cheeks,

so sweet as she smiles, giggles, and replies, "You so crazy, you a *freak.*"

Cootchie Fresh

It is very pleasant when a sister is cootchie fresh, meaning that she is clean

between her legs. However, some women do not know the meaning of body or

feminine spray.

Let's face it, folks: we all sweat as adults, and it is not cool for a man or a woman

not to be fresh below the waist. When you are in a meaningful relationship,

by all means a man or woman who is not fresh below the waist is not cool;

however when they are smelling good, it is a soothing situation.

When you are in a meaningful relationship, by all means a man or woman

at some point might want to perform oral pleasures. You do not want to smell

some *oh hell no* or upset your partner's stomach. So, my people, please keep

your crotch cootchie fresh.

You Done Started Something You Can't Finish

You talk so much tease talk, that's what your mouth says.

In fact, can you back up what you say? Is it just pillow talk?

Walk, baby. Shake those hips when you come in my presence.

Your essence is my presence; your beauty makes me glow inside.

There is nothing like a Black woman, so don't tell your woman

that you will turn her out and not finish the job.

Women love to be finessed, financed, and secured. Once you start small talk

and foreplay with a woman, perhaps those secretions and juices begin to

flow, and, yes, when that time is right, indeed yes, be ready, guys, because that woman

will unleash a pot of sexy steam that will rock your *dreams*.

Always be prepared to have a romantic dinner, take her out to a nice show, and

let her know that she is your *queen* and you are her *king*. Always start something

that you can finish.

Mind Your Business

No matter where you go, where you are, there is always someone

in your business. The old folks always said, "You have six months to

mind your business, and six more months to stay out of everyone else's
business."

People who gossip, constantly mixing with people's relationships or
affairs,

need to get a grip.

Some people break up relationships and marriages by giving

too much advice; hence, some people should learn from experience.

We can't fix everyone's problems.

Sometimes we should fall back,

stand back, and just let people take care of their own personal business.

At times it is not appropriate to get involved with a situation;

however, you must use common sense to know when it is the right time
to step in and

help someone. Your business should be your goals, your objectives, and
of course

your family. The amount of time it takes to mind someone else's business is a waste of energy; on the other hand, if you use your time wisely

to take care of your own business, you don't have to worry about your business

taking care of you.

Consciously think positive, believe, assume, move powerfully, and always

make it your business to succeed, position yourself to achieve, and always

stay in a structured lane to excel.

Voting Matters

Everyone who is qualified to vote or registered to vote should vote.

Your vote matters because everyone needs these:

1. **Equality,** which gives every American an opportunity to have a voice and a fair chance

2. **Jobs,** which are what keep families, the economy, and our existence relevant and successful

3. **Health care,** which keeps more families, companies, and single households safe and healthy

4. **Education,** which makes Americans more prepared for and successful in the job market

5. **The stock market,** which gives Americans an advantage in investments, great financial potential, and a bright, successful future

6. **The auto industry,** which is imperative to put quality cars on the road to make friends, family, and corporations happy and successful

7. **Social Security,** which provides a better equality of life through both small and big companies

We all know that the economy matters in the way that we budget, manage, and expand our finances to keep ourselves succeeding and moving forward.

Count your options, count your goals and objectives, count your family's future,

count your anticipated success, and count your vote.

Weavalicious

Yes, that sister is weavalicious, beautiful, essential, and sexy.

Do not talk about her, because, yes, she bought that hair and, yes, she is claiming it.

When a sister gets her "hair did," and she knows it is done well, truly every brother

on the scene will turn his head and say, "Wow, Miss, you look so freaking good."

In the hood, sisters wear weaves for various reasons each season;

in fact, some women color their hair to gain a better head of hair.

No matter what the case may be, weaves in various colors bring

a certain sex appeal to a woman, making her desirable to a man of

caliber.

So, brothers, never dis a sister with a weave, because her ratchet side

will bust you out. Honey blonde, cherry, honey brown, jet black, or silver blonde—

there are different colors of weaves and various styles—short, medium,

or long. All divas, stand up and strut your sexy self. Whether you wear a heel, pump, or wedge, by all means you never miss a beat with your cute

earrings, makeup, outfit, and beautiful smile.

When you go out and heads turn, just remember that being weavalicious

is a lesson for those divas who have turned their man with style, finesse, and excitement.

The First of Each Month

In the hood, in a joking way people refer to the first of each month

as Mother's Day, meaning that's the day mothers receive food stamps or other

supplemental income from the city, county, or state. However, I think this

is not a joking matter, because there are people who really need help. At the same

time, it is imperative that people that get assistance eventually attend school

and do a workforce program to enhance their life as well as elevate their

family's social status.

There are a lot of businesses that accept the family-first card (EBT or debit card).

There was a time when people could not use a food stamp card in small Latin

grocery stores (*bodagas*) or dollar stores. Perhaps today is a new opportunity

to shop smart, save, and make your source of income stretch from month to month.

People who choose to get high may not value or budget their money, because

their first priority is to do drugs.

Damn! It's the first of the month. Wow! My stamps came before the fifth.

Well, anyway, downtown has hella people, and the buses are so damn crowded.

Businesses are rich from the first to the fifth of each month. My late mother

received public assistance when I was a child, and I was never ashamed to

go to the store with food stamps. And, by the way, we did not have cards

at that time; it was food-stamp cash. Nevertheless, appreciate what

you have today, and prepare to build a smarter tomorrow.

Gangster Boo in the Hood

No matter where you go in this country, and regardless of what city, county, or

hood, there is always a gangster boo in your hood. A gangster boo

is a sister in a city that always has your back, no matter what.

She is a chick that is outspoken, strong minded, and calculating

when making decisions.

Men, if you choose to have a gangster boo, by all means,

You'd better man up when she needs your support financially, mentally, physically,

or spiritually. A gangster boo is a fly girl and is always on point with her hair, nails,

clothes; she has a vicious boot and shoe game.

Men in the hood, respect a gangster boo that takes care of her kids and

her man and at the same time can make you laugh, turn you on, and have you saying, "Wow,

what a woman!" all in the same moment.

There are gangster boos of all kinds, Some are professional women who know how to turn the switch off and on when the time is appropriate.

I take my hat off with the most respect to women who stand their ground and

achieve what is appropriate for themselves and their family.

The Hoop in the Hood

There's nothing like a good game of rock, which how we refer to as basketball in our home

neighborhood. There are no RFs, as there would be in a high school, college, or

pro game. Many guys dunk, do fancy dribbles, smack the ball, steal the ball,

block shots, and there is always excitement inside the paint—and, yes, a *big man*

who is anxious to dunk under the hoop off a quick pass. You must understand

that hood basketball involves unity, discipline, and teamwork.

There are one-on-ones, two-on-twos, three-on-threes, and full court,

five-on-fives, and horse, where there is follow-the-leader. No matter what age you are,

perhaps you've never stopped having a love for the sweet game of basketball.

Get Your Drink on the Spot in the Club

Everywhere you go, there is a club that keeps a great party in effect.

Let's keep it real: a great party is definitely kept by a powerful DJ.

Get your groove on, get your swirl on, get your mack on, get your party on, and

just hit it on the beat. Light or dark alcohol, wine or beer—get your drink on, and drink responsibly.

Never drink and drive, and always have a designated driver to take you home

if you are to have several drinks.

There are plenty of sexy ladies in a club;

carefully choose one. Consequently, there are many types in a club:

stalkers, playgirls, playerettes, serious, sexy, groupies, independents,

gold diggers, and last but not least, keepers.

Some women like when men buy them a drink, but they know who

is deserving before you do that favor, men. Everyone, when you drink in the club, know how to play your cards if you want to date someone

from the club. And, yes, sometimes you can hit the jackpot and score with

a nice, sweet pretty lady.

Silver Spoon, Silver Cup

There are a variety of earned incomes in the hood. You can have a family living in an apartment building and in the same block or

neighborhood living different lifestyles. People of color have different goals,

objectives, passions, beliefs—and definitely not the same attitudes.

Unfortunately, across America, there are a lot of single-parent homes; nevertheless, some people like to drive nice cars and live in nice homes, and

other people prefer taking the bus and living in an apartment. However, at the

same time, they take a lavish vacation when needed.

We all know that everyone was not born with a silver spoon or a silver cup.

All children in the education system should be encouraged to build a career or education or trade post-graduation. There is so much negativity, violence,

hate, and low self-esteem in the hood. At this point, each generation will become

stronger through self-esteem, confidence, encouragement, discipline, and motivation.

Survival is a must in the hood, and you know that everything you want you

must earn. If you want to succeed, without a doubt faith and self-control will always

keep you out in front, and you will never have to give up or quit, because your choice

today can give you a bright tomorrow.

Morning Sex

The best sex is early in the morning, when you get the best rest at night

and those juices just marinade—indeed a sweet storage for bedroom passion and

enjoyment. Sex all night is enjoyable as well, but all sex is never the same.

Perhaps it depends on your sex partner, your connection, and your dynamic chemistry.

Guys wake up with a boner, ready to bone her. Kisses are

so wet as he kisses and licks her all over her sexy body. She melts as he licks on

her nipples and sucks away on the beat as she moans through a passionate speech.

Tell your lady good morning after great sex in the morning as she "takes a tinkle"

and you drain the "main vein." Ahh, what a relief, nodding your head in spectacular

belief, saying "You were great." Nevertheless, breakfast after sex is the best.

Foreplay all night sets up a slam-dunk for powerful, passionate morning sex, touching each other in all the right places, making ooh-ahh faces.

Right there, biting your lip, scratching back hot, juicy, wet, banging sex.

Those walls are saying, "If we only could talk," as her walls are saying,

"Oh baby, right there."

Keep It Real

In the African-American community, if you get in someone's face in the

hood with some nonsense, believe me, they will go up top. Perhaps you know

what it is, fool. For those thorough chicks that want the best, don't mess with

a guy who is all talk. Tell them, "Kick rocks, sucker."

Ladies have to get that money and tell him to haul ass and take a hike.

Remember, people, time is money, and money is time. Ladies and gentlemen,

you have what it takes to succeed. Don't let anyone block your blessings,

opportunities, or *future*. Build on what you have accomplished. Keep it one

hundred. Don't half-step. Step up your game. Put on your game face. And maintain

a successful name.

Fashion Is Paramount in the African-American Community

People judge you on first impressions. Indeed, first impressions can be

lasting impressions. Self-esteem stays high when you are clean and

when you wear clothing that is in style. Daily you will attract pleasant compliments.

When someone compliments you, say "Thank you for the compliment." The response will be "You're welcome." Attractive skin, nails,

and hair are effective fashion tools in the African-American community.

There is unity among fashion-conscious people, and color stands out with attitude,

walking down the runway of the catwalk, sidewalk, or workplace.

There is a smile on your face because you are color-coordinated and

designer down. Remember, the clothes don't make you; perhaps your personality

is your best fashion statement.

You Are Just Mad

Do not keep anger bottled up; express yourself. Do not be jealous.

When you are just mad as hell, talk to someone about what you are upset about. In fact,

get it off your chest; don't hate or hesitate. You can't be aggy or aggravating;

this is not cool. Don't play yourself or fade yourself; you must not act the fool.

Remember, in twelve years of school, we are here to learn, but

sometimes our emotions get out of control as inside we start to burn.

You are just mad as hell because they are doing better than you. What are we to do?

We must have gratitude and appreciate what we have and build every day

as we pray. Turn your frown into a smile, and blessings will come your way.

Be patient; in a little while, you will say, "I am no longer mad."

Your anger can't exist as long as you have confidence, and your motivation will always keep a smile on your face. Thus, mad energy also can't exist when

there is love, passion, and excitement about a solution that you are prepared to use.

Books Bring Knowledge

Reading is rudimental, experimental, experiential, and fundamental.

We as a people must seek knowledge and wisdom daily.

Elevation, preservation, and education will keep you more informed.

History brings knowledge through culture, family values, and awareness. In addition

to Black history, without a doubt there are inventors, writers, leaders,

teachers, doctors, lawyers—and being the first people on the planet.

Research is knowledge; research through reading brings great knowledge and

awareness, giving you confidence and power to keep you successful.

A book can provide information on nutrition, history, novelty, spirituality,

drama/suspense, or love/suspense.

Reading can also help build vocabulary as well as introduce great

conversation. Knowledge comes from different outlets: talk radio, the Internet,

newspapers, magazines, and CD books. Fill your home with great books;

introduce easy reading to youths, and encourage your family to seek knowledge.

Stay open-minded and on course to improving your thinking daily.

Lastly, critical thinking can be your best weapon; always keep learning

as your best opportunity.

Ratchet on the Job

In the hood you always get someone who acts ratchet—out of pocket,

ghetto with an attitude—or who just don't care if anyone gets upset when they do something

disrespectful, like when you are on the city bus and someone gets on the bus, talking

loud on his cell phone, and sits directly behind you and speaks at the top

of his lungs.

I never like it when people only want to hang out with me or call me when

they think I have money. A true friend is there for you

through thick or thin. Ratchetness is real, and when you deal with people who are

fake and never real or true to good morals and values, it's a problem.

Folks who yell out at night for people when their doorbell and cell phone

works are just ridiculous. Never go to the club with the intention of getting real drunk

and starting fights; you might get your ass handed to you.

Ratchetness does have consequence, though at time it is comical, and in some

circumstances it can be embarrassing.

Some people are so unhappy, they will not stop until others around

them are feeling the same negative energy. Positive energy gets rid of ratchet

people, so if you want power, prosperity, and good presence,

you must surround yourself with that activities.

Run ratchet folk away, and never stoop to ignorance. Indeed, take the

high road and always stand your ground. Do your job and live with

good intentions. Pray, love, respect, restore, build, and succeed.

Feel the Vibe

You must feel the vibes of the people that you keep in your circle, because if they

have big beefs in the street, you can be guilty by association. Love

yourself, know yourself, feel yourself, and push yourself to the next level. Always

think forward and never backward.

Positive vibrations always connect people; great compliments affect

people. Assume leadership, and inspire people. Colors, numbers, and objects

have vibrations, and independence gives you the best feeling and vibe

inside. Indeed, this is the best satisfaction that someone can achieve.

This, That, and the Third

Everyone in every hood has heard this terminology at one point or another:

"This, that, and the third." It means that there is always some drama occurring and that

nonsense seems to always find a way to materialize. People who have

problems sometimes struggle to find solutions when they are frustrated. When

they try to resolve a situation peacefully, ratchet folks find a way to

throw dirt and sand on their plate. The subject at hand—something simple or petty—becomes

a big issue; that is the reason people

stay in ratchet mode. There are at least three variables—

first, second, and third parties—when any hood issue needs a resolution.

No one ever says this, that, the third, and the fourth. Language is very rhythmic, and

it's essential to observe body language because

a person's body language will tell you how he or she feels.

"This, that, and the third" does not always have to end with dissatisfaction and aggravation; common ground can be met and a solution perhaps

will cause laughter and excitement.

Lastly, if something bothers you, get it off your mind and

speak up, because communication and expression can get your pressure under control.

Turn This Party All the Way Out

All African-Americans at some point have partied until they could not stop.

No matter where you go out to party and get your club on—college or celebration parties,

or a club scene, there is always a sexy lady ready to get her groove on. You can't bring

everybody and anybody to your house, because some people will see your assets,

set you up, and rob you clean.

People should have a good time when they go out, but

be responsible: drink responsibly, think responsibly, and appreciate life's fun and

opportunities. There is no need to pretend to be something that you are not.

When you keep it real, that's a turn-on and so hot.

Turn Me on Until the Break of Dawn

Lady, turn me on nonstop; kiss me passionately with your hot juicy lips;

talk sexy things in my ear. Baby, you have me wide open; it feels good

all over. Turn on some sexy, get-us-in-the-mood music.

Chocolate candy and kisses, whipped cream, sweet conversation, without

hesitation, wet lips, sexy hips, juicy thighs, and light-brown eyes.

Every month is Valentine's, and keeping things grown and sexy is always

the agenda. Spanking, moaning, groaning, and "if only these walls could tell

the story."

Man Up with a Woman's Touch

Men are masculine, and women are feminine. Moreover, men are rational,

and women are emotional. Men who respect themselves, love themselves, motivate

themselves, and accept responsibility will always man up.

Men succeed more with the support of a strong woman. A woman's touch always

has the most finesse and success in decorating the home, cooking nutritious food,

making passionate love, and giving sound advice and unconditional love.

Men, take care of your children and family, and if possible, help your

relatives. You must know when it is appropriate to help and also when to fall

back and not let anyone take advantage of you.

Motivation Right, Haters Left

Get out my way, haters.

Do not hang with haters. Haters left as

your motivation became right. Haters can't stay in your company; nevertheless,

do not invite haters. Perhaps there is nobody home; please get off the premises

with all that negativity. Because you are mad or sad, it seems like a problem.

Your motivation is here, and your presence is so positive and powerful.

Remember, light and darkness do not coexist;

your energy is the light, and your prayers are light, and your brilliance is light.

People must stay on a high frequency and also stay motivated. In addition, people

are always watching, but you must give them higher standards to follow and

always be thankful daily: waking up, eating a meal, having a place to stay and clothes on your back

and great health as well as strength.

Haters are just mad because they want to think negative and be somebody

too. Subsequently even a hater can change his or her life around and become positive—

and can even become a motivator. Think motivation, feel motivation, believe in and understand

motivation, and most of all, stay motivated.

She Keeps It on Lock

A real sister, meaning a true Black woman or woman

of any race, will keep her man's best interests at heart.

At the same time, she will call, occasionally checking up on her man

to make sure there are no other women trying to get their claws

on him.

This beautiful Black female is confident in the way that she

messages, cooks, cleans, and always gives a throw-down love performance

in the bedroom. Sister Black female, please keep your guard up,

as you already know there is a shortage of good Black men.

There's a Solution When Negativity Attacks

One must remember that kindness always irritates negative people.

You must smile and laugh at people who despise you. When you have light,

people who are in darkness never want to stay in the light.

There is a spiritual war going on in the world, and we must realize that in

when we take it to the next level, we receive resistance.

Prayer and meditation are the best solution when any type of enemy

attacks. Love and confidence always defeat fear and negativity.

Connect the Dots to All Your Valid Points

All points that make sense always connects, and when you are in agreement,

valid points always seem to connect. Everyone does not always agree on the same

point, but with common ground, both parties can find a way to make

goals happen. People must know that listening is a powerful weapon, and silence

is golden; nevertheless always observe, think, and work diligently so you can be

successful.

When you want to get things accomplished, unfortunately, not everyone will

be happy that you want to succeed. We must think straight

as a people and not let things escalate. But with people—adults or

kids—someone has to be the bigger person and walk away. Never look down,

talk down to, or disrespect others. Without hesitation, be humble, build what you have, appreciate what is granted, and meditate your way toward every situation

or decision that you encounter.

Never lose your mind or do anything or say anything that you might

regret. Keep your thinking straight; keep your mind right

and your body tight.

Stop Blocking

There are so many people in cities that do not want you to achieve, succeed, and proceed ahead. You have cock blocking, blessing blocking, player haters, ratchetness, and just plain negativity in the hood's atmosphere.

Never block yourself from a great opportunity; with a positive attitude, you

can receive and achieve more in the long run. People who are loud, rude, and

nasty toward you cannot expect you to owe them any type of favor.

Respect is reciprocal, meaning it is a two-way street. When someone

misses out on an opportunity because of a bad attitude, they can't get mad at the

world but must realize that they are blocking themselves.

Stay focused and keep

your attitude optimistic.

Family First

Men and women, ladies and gentlemen, always take care of home first, meaning

bills, children, and spiritual, mental, emotional, and financial priorities. By all means, have

your priorities in place with a plan of action. A family that works together, bonds,

and prays will always stay a unit. We all know that families might have disagreements

at times; however, with a balance of judgment, communication, and commitment,

your family can make things work. Women should never put a man

in front of their children, and a man should always take care of his kids before he

takes care of another woman's kids. Remember, *family first,* and everything

will always be a blessing.

Girl, You Got It Going On

I love those hips, those sweet hips, pussy so deep, so juicy, it puts me to sleep.

Girl, I love those juicy lips so delicious, so tasty; just give me a kiss, and I will say,

"Mmm, so nice." Kiss me all over and say it's good. I think it's nice the way

you look so sexy, the way you talk and walk, your fly personality. I love a Black

woman that has a little ghetto and a lot of class, nice breasts and a big ass.

Black women love compliments all day as they wear it on their sleeves.

Keep a Black woman happy, and she will always be your best friend. Just remember,

Black men, always tell your lady, "You have it going on."

The Hustle on the Block

A yo! they on the block; they got their hustle on the block; they have

a lookout on the block. The block have their paper up; the block is where they

be at, and if you dare try to come in and take over, trust and believe, there will be

a price to pay.

There is respect on the block, and there is love and unity on the block.

Wow, there is a lot of heads on the block, and their stash is not known, so do not

snitch and play them out, because if it was legal, trust and believe they would

pay taxes on it.

You Met Your Match

There is always somebody bigger and better or badder than you.

Perhaps you should always carefully pick which battle is appropriate to fight.

However just because someone is stronger than you does not mean you have

to be a coward and back down. People might not like you, but they will respect

you. In addition, we as people of color should always stay on point and stand

our ground.

You should never go around picking fights. Staying

humble will get you a lot further than being a target of the hood or society,

marked for trouble. Remember, God is the most powerful, and we should

always keep him first.

Once Upon a Time Where I Grew Up

I was born in the late sixties and grew up in the seventies and eighties. Perhaps those

were the good old days when children really respected their elders and you

could walk the streets without worrying about violence or ignorance.

Unfortunately we live in a time now when a child will curse an adult out without thinking

about it.

No matter what, each generation should get stronger and not weaker—yes

smarter through technology but also through common sense and *respect*.

When I attended college in the nineties, the experience made

me what I am today: determined, ambitious, motivated, and successful.

Delaware State University and the US Marine Corps, thank you

for making me a well-rounded machine that exemplifies prosperity

to the community.

No More Excuses

People of color should never make excuses, because we have so many

opportunities in this country through work, education, and entrepreneurship.

We as people of color can't blame our problems on foreigners or get mad,

because we must have a thirsty drive daily to achieve the impossible, conquer

the invisible, and move any roadblock.

Always push yourself to be better day by day, and always build yourself.

Avoid mistakes from your past. There is power in prayer, confidence,

motivation, and determination. Without a doubt, you can accomplish

your goals and objectives. People of color should never blame the world or

make excuses for mistakes that have been made. Furthermore, with a

plan of action, you will move forward in the right direction.

If you are not looking for trouble, perhaps you should not start trouble,

because who and what you surround yourself with can effect you, whether for bad or for good. Moreover, keep yourself surrounded by powerful, motivating,

stimulating, and cultivating individuals who lead by example and

succeed by motion.

Words are powerful, and your diction should contain words

like I can, I will, in time I will be able to, in God's will, etc. Remember you can be

successful in life. No more excuses!

Realizing Your Strength

Everyone has potential; nevertheless, we all have different stress levels.

In addition to that, we must

learn to relax, relate, and resist negativity. Build where you are weak, and add

where you are strong. Always learn from others by observing and asking

questions. Analyze every situation, and build your hypotheses.

An educated guess can help you, and research will give you reassurance.

Mentally and physically, we must remain fit and strong and never give up or quit.

Surround yourself with potential. Start at day one, when it is

just a thought, and make the first step at day one, without hesitation.

Pace yourself at a steady rate, and in time you will reap great benefits through

hard work, patience, and persistence. Next we can all learn and adapt from

other people's strengths, and we can definitely learn to sidestep to avoid the pitfalls of other people's weaknesses. In order to become stronger, we must

never deny any of our faults or mistakes but make changes and do the things

that are necessary to succeed.

Doing Wrong Will Not Make You Right

People in cities, regardless of their nationality, have to realize

that if you always think of a scheme to get over, eventually consequences

will follow. Robbing, stealing, or hurting someone in any fashion

can create bad karma for any individual. Remember that what you do to

people, right or wrong, will come back to you sevenfold.

Position your thinking and yourself to do good; help

someone in need, and do things that will keep you out of trouble and keep

you successful. There is power in love, respect, and self-respect.

Lastly, do things that are right, stay strong, and never give up the fight.

Getting the Draws

Guys always brag about getting the draws; nevertheless, should guys kiss and tell? In fact, most women do not like it when guys put their business out there. What can really get the guys some draws is respect, showing love, and taking care of their lady when she really needs help. Thus, getting the draws—or as some men say, "the panties"—means foreplay is very necessary, just as are surprising her with gifts,

dinner, movies, or a nice trip to some romantic or exotic venue.

Always appreciate a good woman, because when you put work toward your lady, she will spend some overtime on you.

Hood Recipe

There are many ingredients that go into a hood, like mentality:

toughness, roughness, always being on guard, and stepping to you if you cross that line.

Territory is an issue because you have to know where you can be and where

you should not be. Consequently, trouble can always find you when you are at

the wrong place at the wrong time.

Thus, there are divas, boos, baby mamas, and drama queens in

the hood. There is never a dull moment in the hood, because there are

people that always keep a hot gossip topic going. There are liquor stores

everywhere in the hood. "Can I get a quarter so I can get drunk? Can I get a

dollar anyway?" There are go-go bars and strip clubs everywhere in the hood,

sexy ladies saying, "You want a lap dance?" "You want to date for a good time?"

You can be successful growing up in the hood; through education,

discipline, and a plan of action, you can live a middle- or upper-class life.

Always be proud of your city; rep your city; travel around the country and to

other parts of the world. People of color must be well-rounded, well versed, and

well traveled. Also stay motivated, connected, and in continuous motion so you

speak and feel great every day. Never let anyone put you down, and always

keep your money up!

Read Success in the Book of Opportunity

Realize what you are born with—your mind—and understand that

to think clearly, you must read and pursue success. Time waits for no one, and

we need to research a situation before we make a decision.

When people envy you, they will go out their way to

upset you. At this junction, you must address it and dismiss them with

kindness. We all know that kindness gets to people.

Reading places you on the road of success. It also

builds your awareness and builds a great vocabulary.

Unisex Shop

In every city, you have a neighborhood barbershop, and an

essence beauty shop. These are places where men and women get

together to discuss current and past topics. Men bring their

children there, and grooming and hot discussions become assumed
items.

When they leave a barbershop or a salon, men and women step

out into their urban neighborhoods looking sharp, fly, smooth, and

ready to succeed in the world. A haircut always gives men confidence;

women look at them and say, "Wow, you look handsome."

Women of color love a variety of hairstyles: dreads, short, natural,
braids,

finger waves, curls, straight, permed, touchups, doobies, or a nice
weave.

Sisters are so entertaining, bold, Black, and beautiful in different

shades: light skinned, red-bone, caramel, chocolate, and dark

skinned, ski-bone, and dark blonde. Our sisters

of color are so beautiful. There are women that maintain their hair, nails, and feet every month; at the same time there are men who go

to the barbershop every week, and as a culture the unisex

shop will always stay, because it keeps people of color looking good

every time.

Bad Black Sister

I love my ebony Nubian queen. Indeed, that Black sister got it

going on: a good job, independent, and knowing what direction she is heading.

No doubt she is the talk of the week. Men, you can't step to her with

weak game. Perhaps, if your game and approach is tight, by all means you

can get a great date with her. The bad Black sister likes to be spoiled,

wined, and dined as well as given the finer things in life.

Our ebony sisters have a variety of goals and objectives; in the same

way there is always a man that will fit their type: thug, conservative, spiritual,

well-balanced comic. You also have that spiritual bad Black sister who seeks

a man that is equally yoked with her, meaning on the same spiritual page.

An ebony Nubian princess will never back down from you, and if she

dares feel you, she will burn in the kitchen and eventually make love to

you in the bedroom. Bad Black sisters are bad to the bone, sassy, and sexy.

They always know what to say, and they always make the right moves when the time is

appropriate.

Never disrespect that bad Black sister, because if you step out of line,

she will verbally knock you out on the spot. African-American women, I

have so much love for you.

Woke Up in Something Good

Brothers in everyhood all have the same goal: to have a fine, foxy woman to wake up to every morning. It is a breath of fresh air to wake up and roll over and smile at a pleasant face, sweet attitude, and clean hygiene. When you have a partner that has banging sex and knows where to touch and what to kiss and grab, without hesitation a smile will appear once again on your face. Talking trash during sex does help heightens your sex drive and adds flavor to your bedroom presentation. Men like sex that is wet, sweet, juicy, moist, sensual, and ever so soft.

Add a romantic bubble bath or sexy shower with all the works and hot oil

to relax the body with a soothing massage.

A man loves to wake up to a great breakfast after a nice night. But

as long as you keep your lady happy, you will stay

satisfied. All men should stay in gear and stay focused on your relationship or friendship and remain a strong man. Then you will always wake up in something good.

A Realization of Who Is Truly *Real*

There is an old saying in the hood: "Real recognizes real."

In other words, if you are not faking who you truly are, surely a strong man

or woman will read this quickly. No matter what, growing up or as an

adult, everyone should be themselves and not go out of their way

to impress their peers.

Never let peer pressure get you into trouble;

be an effective leader, not a lost follower. Discover your

strength as a man of color. Always be proud of where you are

from and where you are headed by all means necessary.

An Ebony Triple Threat

In any urban society, I am proud to say, we have ebony

triple threats: Black, beautiful, and intelligent. Needless to say,

we have a lot of people who successfully own their own business,

home, condo, loft, or estate. Black men and women who can think

powerfully build their community and family and always sustain

continued respect, trust, and ambition.

Speak confidently with a varied vocabulary; words

are powerful and speak things into existence. Men and women both seek

happiness: a good mate, a good job or career, and someone who is

dependable through good time and hard times. In order to live a healthy
life,

one must eat, exercise, and think in a healthy fashion.

Create the spiritual context to succeed: pray or meditate daily, budget your

finances, and treat yourself every quarter, once your bills are paid.

People of color must choose their mates carefully. Waiting for the

right match can make your life wonderful, your days happy, and your
years joyful.

Salute to the Hood

I have great respect for Black men in the hood that hold it down:

block, corner, turf, family, and home. It is not easy growing up in low-income housing.

Just because you are from the hood

certainly does not mean you can't be successful.

I salute those in the hood because of the respect that is earned.

cities have their methods of survival, and by all means never sleep on

any city in the United States or around the world. Never let people run, game,

scam, play out, or fade you at any level. Most importantly,

perhaps you should mind your own business when it come to things that do not concern you.

On the Bus

There is so much amazing stuff on the bus.

There are people—perhaps a small percentage—that will look for a way not to

pay their bus fare. "Does anyone have change for a twenty?" Mind you,

they had ample time to get change from the

store behind them. "Does anyone want a two-zone bus card for

twenty-five dollars?" Keep in mind that bus card is fake.

When you get on the bus and flash a fake card, not every bus

driver will let you slide.

Hustlers are on the bus too. "I got that new bootleg movie, two for five!"

The most irritating thing on the bus in a city is when people

are on their cell phones shouting and cursing people out when they need to

take it down and wait until they get off the bus. Very

ratchet. There are thugs on the bus, too, baby mamas on the bus, little

ones saying, "Can I keep the bus paper from the machine?" Daily there is always some type of activity on the bus. "Next stop, please! How much is it

for a transfer?"—even though most people know and catch the bus daily.

In the winter it's freezing at the bus stop. "Wow, where is the bus?"

I just *know* that bus driver did not say, "Move back. The bus is overcrowded. Please wait for the next one."

No Disease, Please

Men and women, understand that there are many diseases

out there. Everyone should strap up with protection and

be careful who you sleep with; consequently, you should get to know

each other first before you have hot, passionate sex. If it smells

stankalicious, believe me, you don't want any part of that funk sauce.

If it is not cool-smelling funkalicious coming through the pants,

you really do not want to welcome any disease.

Sex Appeal

Sex appeal is a must in the hood, so women accent

their looks through makeup, urban fashion, earnings, tattoos, piercings,

extended eyelashes, weaves, extensions, etc. Men hit the gym or

improve themselves on the block with lifting weights, push-ups, pull-ups, and

sit-ups to impress the ladies in the hood. But what truly gives a man

or a woman sex appeal is stability, discipline, good character, faith, and

common sense. Sex appeal requires having a great personality, being clean, smelling good,

and keeping yourself hot and ever so desirable. Hygiene is a must: nice

teeth, clean hair, and cool breath. Sex appeal is learned from parents, peers,

television, radio, and movies. Choose your style,

be yourself, and keep it real.

Checkoff

We all must be prepared for whatever comes our way.

In music, a checkoff happens after you have practiced your music,

art, or dance, and you audition or show your work to see if you know your stuff.

In the workforce, you should know everyone's job, so if there is a

posting for a promotion, you will be ushered to the next level

without hesitation.

People are always judged on their appearance, actions, and

character, so always stay consistent, keep your word, and by all

means, finish what you started. Be proactive and not reactive,

and accept constructive criticism with open arms.

Morning Rush

I woke up this morning, thankful and grateful to see another day. Seeing each day motivates me to be better than I was the previous day. Rain, snow, or shine, we must earn a living, and having health and strength gives us a daily rush. Waking up to a person you love is wonderful, and a balanced breakfast can render

a morning rush.

Start your day off right with an optimistic approach. Be strong, confident, and focused on your daily goals. Great sex in the morning

before work gives you a boost of energy and will definitely put a delicious smile on your face.

Bulletproof Plan

In life you want to build a nest egg with savings, checking, a 401k, money

markets, stocks, bonds, etc., to establish stability for the short and the long term. Perhaps

living from check to check just keeps you barely out of the red. Unfortunately,

emergencies do occur, and you need to have

a plan A. So you work overtime and invest your time and money toward your

present circumstance in addition to your future. Your plan B is your backup,

alternative plan of action, which gives you options, such as at what rate you decide to

save and when it is necessary to spend. We all know that money does

not contain happiness alone, but wisdom and common sense can ensure you

a smile and help you avoided headaches and *trouble*.

There are not too many lucky breaks in life, so

when a window to success presents itself, you should attain

your positive goals without hesitation. The world is not in debt to anyone; thus

we all must strive for excellence and always keep the course in front of us at

all times. Strategic thinking is a weapon; learning and listening is a

weapon, and having patience is a position of discipline. Think like a winner, and

take charge of your life. A plan can't work unless you put

it into motion.

Bring Back the Neighborhood

What happened to the good neighbors in our neighborhoods? Shouldn't everyone that lives around you be at least slightly acquainted with each other? Consequently, all neighborhoods are not exactly safe to live in. Nevertheless, you must be friendly at some level in order to function safely where you live. Children must respect their elders, youths must protect the elderly, and those who know the way must teach the young right from wrong.

While this may be true, we at some point must step back and let our youths make some decisions for themselves. In churches, preachers teach and preach, "Love your neighbor, pray for your neighbor, do not envy your neighbor or involve yourself with your neighbor's wife or husband."

Some neighborhoods in our country are

safe, friendly, and gated. No matter where

you live, it is imperative to know who lives around

you. As I grew up in the seventies and eighties, mothers

and grandmothers looked out for other neighbors' kids.

When we build a strong block, a strong avenue,

and a strong community, moving forward we can have a

beautiful country.

Lastly, bring back fun, bring back excitement,

bring back prayer, bring back love, bring back jobs,

bring back Black-owned businesses, and most importantly,

bring good neighbors back to *every hood*.

Liquid Consciousness

In every hood, there is a liquor store

on every corner. People of color must be liquid conscious,

meaning they drink water, milk, and juice to keep their bodies pure and healthy.

The body is made up of mostly of water; we should

not place a lot of alcohol in our system, because alcohol weakens

the mind and dehydrates the body.

Discipline, love, respect, and a strong will keep us from

interacting with this depressant. Alcohol affects the

kidney and liver, and it destroys families and careers. Build your

system with water, vitamins, and nutrition, because you are

what you eat, drink, and think. No matter what, stay motivated,

dedicated, health conscious, spiritual, and most

importantly, liquid conscious.

Wireless Up

You can go to any hood across America and see

someone with a cell phone, iPhone, iPad, iPod, laptop,

etc. Our youth text many characters per day to express what

they are going through at the moment. In contrast, no matter

what you communicate through—the Internet, a phone, or by word of

mouth—it is imperative that you keep a tight connection with

the people in your circle. Email, fax, Skype, Priority

Mail, and inner-office mail are necessary in business in order to communicate,

financially succeed, and recruit staff.

If you are not connected through fiber-optics, it will be very

difficult to build a strong financial or social network in order to

to stay current and consistent to succeed in the world of business.

Ignorant to the Third Power

People are ignorant when they are not aware of what they are interacting with. Some people in the hood and in some places of business might be aware of what is appropriate yet still do things that are rude, wrong, unlawful, and plain, outright ratchet and disrespectful. People who are ignorant to the second power associate only with people who think in a negative way. Folks who are ignorant to the third power look for bad things to involve themselves with: crime, gossip, negative thinking, and poor planning. Be yourself, and never follow negative crowds.

Men, pull your pants up, man up, handle your business, and take no shorts from no one. Some people are about nothing; unfortunately, they have no goals and love to see drama day in and day out. Stop the nonsense; get away from negative circles, and run to powerful ones. When you are about goals and going places, you can influence and inspire people to do

outstanding things. Make your mark in your hood with good, and

never quit on friends who truly require your help. Lastly,

build family, and increase your success daily.

Be About Your Own Business

Always try to be on time; move forward;

do not think backward; bust people out who do not respect you;

don't procrastinate; stay focused and about your business.

Handle your business; take opportunities when a

promotion comes. Blessings are proof that it is your time to shine.

Stay humble. Never forget where you came

from. Likewise, help others in their marriages, friendships,

and employment, or in your own business. There is a time to chill out,

bug out, and shout out, but when it comes to making money, separate

the business from the personal.

Timetable

Once upon a time in the hood, there was a mother

who raised many children as best she could.

Each kid she empowered with a different assignment and

skill. As her kids became older, as

a result of her teaching, they knew how to survive by cooking,

cleaning, being independent, and having a good work ethic.

So her children helped take care of their mother as she

became older.

A mother who cooks great food and places it on the table

will only multiply enjoyment in return. Teach children the right way

to go, and they will not struggle to succeed when they

become adults.

Men who use their time wisely can maximize,

achieve, and sustain success. Never let anyone waste your time,

because time is valuable, and "time waits for no man."

Never wait until the last minute; prepare yourself in

advance. Indeed, preparation makes you a winner every time.

The common denominators of success are prayer, wisdom, patience, and persistence. Plant any seed of opportunity, and in time it will grow. On every table should be good food, family discussions, love and affection, good television and radio, prayer, meditation, and job opportunities. Nevertheless, always plan wisely, utilize your time wisely, and never take any opportunity for granted.

Grown-Ass Woman

She's a grown-ass woman. Yes, this woman is from

the hood and has her own place stacked with

groceries. She is sweet with her wardrobe and also smooth with

her shoe game. This sister can call her own shots and has the

best situation, meaning she does not have to ask anyone for

anything: man or woman.

Grown-ass women hang in groups and pairs, sexy as

can be, so irresistible to the thugs and the intellects in the

hood. Baby ebony boo is so diverse in her style of dress

and hairstyles. If you say anything ratchet to her, *pow!*

she will shoot you down with her looks and follow up with

a strong dis. Grown-ass women are everywhere:

Southern belles, Northeast divas, Midwest mammies,

and don't forget West Coast vixens. Our sisters of the

hood take pride in the way they look: getting their hair

"did" and done, nails manicured and pedicured,

keeping up with hairstyles every month.

Grown-ass women love to travel and take care of their families at home. Only real women understand and socialize with grown-ass women, because they will fight for what's right as well as provide security, food, clothing, and shelter for their kids in the process.

Black women across America, stay Black, bold, and beautiful.

Turned All the Way Out

Sex is essential in every relationship; thus we all

at some point seek a partner or mate who makes our toes

curl up, giving us goose bumps up our arms and a sensational chill down

our back. Next, mentally connecting with someone who is on the

same page, chapter, and level makes anyone satisfied on many

levels. Moreover, when those bells and whistles go off in your

mind, you say to yourself, "Oooh wee, yes, that's it. Right there,

baby, right there." When a woman is wet and a man is at attention,

well, folks, we have a match.

Again, when that sexy feeling hits you, resembling that great

sensational experience, you turn down the lights,

as you are turned all the way out. Men, kiss

your lady passionately in all the right spots; keep her hot, moaning,

begging, and wanting you inside her with full exotic force. Mix up your

lovemaking with your lady. In fact, when you exert different speeds—

slow and screwed, moderate and fast, pounding—no doubt any woman

will cum all over the place and will keep a pretty smile on her face.

Keep excitement in your sex life; stay creative and open-minded,

and without a doubt you will be a great sex partner for life.

A Day at the Park

It is so refreshing to spend a day at the park: quality time walking, jogging, or playing a wholesome game of baseball or basketball. Near the back of the field, you may see a group of men playing a fun game of soccer or golf.

You hear the voices of children running, playing, and enjoying the fruits

and labor of childhood and youth. Adults might curl up with a book, have a picnic or cookout, and enjoy a day of family fun. On holidays there might be a carnival at the park or a great concert to sit back and enjoy. There are fraternities, motorcycle gangs, city gangs, and a community of families that look forward to a happy time at the park for a day.

There are flashy cars as well as family cars, vans, and sport utility vehicles at the park. It's a great place to read, write, and prolifically think. Couples come to the park to bond, enjoy music, and enjoy a great meal. The smell of hotdogs, burgers, ribs, fish, and other foods make your mouth water.

There are plenty of refreshments: water, juice, soda, and alcoholic beverages.

Family reunions are at the park, concluding when the

weather is nice. Please come out and enjoy a good time at your

local park.

Act Wrong

There are so many people in the hood who at times

choose to act wrong, be disrespectful, and just plain not care

who gets upset. Nearby, surrounding their ignorance, is

always someone that has their ass on radar. By any means,

it is guaranteed that when you jump in someone's face with bullshit—

make no mistake—you will be given "some act right."

Your Boo

All guys and gals in the hood have someone dear to
their heart or someone they used to date that was close
to them. Conversely, you have
a variety of situations: your boo, boo-stank, stanka-boo,
sweetheart, sweetie, sweetie pie, honey, queen,
diva, Nubian princess. No matter what, this is definitely
someone who is a girlfriend, wife, boyfriend, or husband.

Men should, from time to time, surprise their lady.
Each month keep your relationship interesting
and possibly move forward to another level. Black women
love to brag about what their boo does for them in comparison.
Black women do compete for affection as proof of instance.
Men love the attention their ladies give and in return keep
their woman smiling.

Men, don't make your boo somebody that's a jump-off; only a true
Nubian princess is worthy of red-carpet

treatment. Your boo will make you a meal when you

handle your business: make money, pay your bills, treat her right. Just be a real man, and stay connected to

what she desires.

Passion for Power

People who seek power position themselves to reach power

through various forms of leadership: legal or illegal, good or bad. When you

work for a corporation, someone at some point will

abuse their position for power. Passion for power is healthy as long

as you have good intentions. Where there is power, there

is responsibility. You have to be thorough, on point,

and determined to develop, strengthen, and motivate those who you are

chosen to lead. Your power is given by God; your strength is given by

our Lord and Savior. We can do all things through pray.

Great power comes from great leaders, and fast

learners become successful at meeting every goal or objective they

encounter. Great listeners also become great leaders. When

you have tolerance, patience, wisdom, and discipline, without a

doubt your passion for power will make you a great leader.

Leaders learn from their mistakes and move forward using

their wisdom to guide others through careful direction.

Your passion is your desire, and power is given through responsibility.

In addition, when you are always consistent and true to what you stand

for morally, you will have a pleasant journey on the avenue of

opportunities.

Lastly, keep your gauges on lock and plenty of motivation on

reserve in your "bank of success."

Baby Mama Hood Drama

Let's face it. Hands down, the queen of the hood is the

baby mama. She will hold her baby father

down as long as he has her back. Baby fathers who choose

to move on have a tendency to sneak and tiptoe to their

baby mothers for love, sex, and affection. Some baby mothers

might have from one to three kids with one man and then have one kid with

another man and then go back to the first baby father.

This baby mama can have the most

control, depending on the circumstance of her relationship with

the children's father. Baby fathers can become husbands, and

baby mamas can become wives. Baby fathers across America

play a major role in the lives of their children.

It is important that they spend quality time with their child;

when they are present, they can make a

positive impact. Women treat men based on how their fathers raise

them, and men treat their women based on how their mothers raised them.

Fathers have to set great examples for children to follow.

Eventually the present generation will be our future adults.

Fatherhood is imperative to help strengthen every home

across America and around the world. Lastly, baby fathers

decrease hood drama and increase family success.

Women of Color, Have Self-Respect

This is dedicated to my sisters of color. After all, self-respect is self-defense from any man.

Self-esteem, strong dreams, and a strong will, desires, and

passion are assumed along with a dynamic personality and fashion.

Black men accept the fact that a sister will be opinionated,

demanding. They expect some drama or just straight-up

honesty. Sisters, stand your ground and hold down the fort.

If a brother chooses outside of the race, I guess it's his

choice. The reason non-Blacks want a sister is

because she is the strongest women on the planet, hands down.

There are women of color in various roles: historians,

our first lady, principals, college presidents, doctors,

ministers, lawyers, congresswomen, judges, athletes, TV hosts,

singers, dancers, actresses, entrepreneurs, millionaires, and

musicians. So our young girls have

a lot to be proud of.

Black History Month is February,

but our sisters of color make history every day. Our grandmothers, mothers, and daughters are three generations strong. Perhaps each generation should teach the next to build unity, strength, confidence, and success. No matter what, I respect all women of color, and women that take care of business—Black or non-Black.

Increase on the Come Up

It is a wonderful feeling when you grew up in

poverty and as an adult finally surface, make good money, and

become successful. My theme is "Just because you are from the hood, that

does not mean you can't succeed." Praise the come up; get down with

the come up; celebrate the come up; party with the come up; support the

come up; do not hate on the come up; never get upset with the come up.

Increase your meditation, and decrease yourself through humble gratitude.

Sustain gratitude; always be thankful for your blessings.

Get paid on your come up; get your bread and paper on your come up.

Never think backward; don't downgrade or degrade yourself. Love and

be yourself. Stand up for yourself. When you work hard toward promotions,

eventually you will attain your goals. Hard work does pay off.

Always take your ambition to the next level. Become a better person every day.

Keep your mind on point and your game face tight.

Never let anyone take advantage of you or walk on you like you

are a nobody. Moreover, work toward excellence, never settling for less.

Every day, give it your all. People might try to place roadblocks in your way, but your

determination will always help you to achieve.

Time Travel

Time and space are essential to life;

thus space starts from the womb. Time is the period

that you are carried in the womb, and of course life

is held inside a mother's womb. We all should

use time wisely. In addition to time apart, space and

compromise help all relationships excel. Always

try your best to be on time; travel at least four times

a year; and make time to create your own

space and have alone time. There is a time and

place for everything. Traveling makes

you aware, refreshes you, and increases the

number of interesting people you will meet.

People say that time travel is possible.

Perhaps, in dream states, people can go to the

future or the past to view certain events.

We all time travel for a reason.

When we dream, we travel while we are

asleep. When we are awake, there might be a slight

imbalance and slight throbbing of the ankles. It is very

dangerous to wake someone while he or she is in transition.

Our sleep state is a reflection of our conscious

thoughts and efforts. Consciousness and awareness

are connected to time; time moves forward and

backward, so it can work for you or

against you if you do not use it wisely. If you had a time

machine, where would you go?

What century or time period would you visit?

Meditation and prayer

should be exercised daily.

We all know that great wealth

is connected to great health. By all means, when you eat

healthy, think healthy, and sustain a balanced schedule

through time management, without a doubt, you can succeed.

People who get paid to travel have an advantage of

exposure. Whether you get to travel by car, bus, rail, or air, time goes by quickly. The travel industry involves anything from lodging to

dining to entertainment. In the cruise industry alone,

there is great variety. Lastly, always pray, no

matter which way you time travel.

Balance

Everything form of life requires checks and
balances, whether on this earth or throughout every
solar system. On this planet, we have good
as well as evil. In addition, there are as many
people for you as against you. So beware.
Financially, we must have a
balanced budget in order for us to have financial
comfort. People in general watch a high volume
of television, but there is a time for
entertainment and a time for reading, family, and
quiet time alone for Think-Tank Quality
Assurance.

Relationships grow when balance is in place:
travel, intimacy, family relationships, spirituality, and most importantly,
business. Time and history dictate all: when there
is balance, people focus on things that are

a great priority, depending on what they need to access

in making their life a happy, comfortable,

common-sense, and hassle-free.

Balance can be executed in sections and also

through compromise; thus balance can equal success,

and success is also equated with sacrifice and discipline.

Our Creator controls everything, everywhere. And

God will have the final say in any situation.

Perhaps we are here to do good, help others, and become

more spiritually conscious of our everyday existence.

Lastly, always humble yourself, and

allow God to increase you every time.

Hood Hair Care

Women of color don't get their hair done.

They just "get it did." When women get

their hair done, they can sweat it out.

When a sister gets her hair "did,"

it sustains its beauty as long as she

keeps it wrapped and maintained. Wash, rinse,

condition, dry, and color are ways to sustain that

diva look.

Men are attracted to women who maintain

a tight and sexy appearance. Women

love a man who smells good, looks good, and keeps

himself well groomed. Beauty is not perceived the

same in everyone's opinion; on the contrary,

there is someone for everyone.

Represent Your Hood

When people try to disrespect you, immediately put them in their place. It's only right according to hood etiquette. Hood etiquette takes a lot of heart, passion, effort, and aggression. People of color in the hood take their family, money, and job or other responsibilities very seriously, so never threaten nor play with anything just mentioned.

No matter where you are from, it does matter where you exist in your goals in reference to where you are succeeding. Be proud of where you are from. Never be ashamed. People around the world will know that you are a great product of society.

African-Americans and diaspora Africans come from various countries on the motherland, Africa, where time began for all races of people. The structure of your nose, ears, and lips is the blueprint of the tree that you are from.

Indeed, good trees bear good fruit, and the motherland

provides a rich history, leadership, and

great technology.

Love your race. Love your skin. Love your mind.

Love being Black without saying, "Black is beautiful."

Black people and people of color in in the United

States, the Caribbean, South America, and Europe

are strong in numbers and represent their hoods above

and beyond.

I was raised in the hood, born in Newark, New

Jersey, better known as Brick City. When I went to

Delaware State University, I met people from

Wilmington, Philly, Detroit, Chicago, DC, Miami,

Brooklyn, and more. I learned about

their ways of life and also learned to respect everyone's

point of view. Most people outside of New Jersey are shocked

when I say Newark, because I do not come

across as a thug. I am viewed as an intellectual, a motivator, a teacher,

and most importantly, a good person to deal with.

Full-Time Lover Part Time

Men and women spend too much time and energy

outside of their relationship with secret companions.

People should spend adequate time with their

mates so that their relationship can flourish. You really should take advantage of time

spent together, when you can build a strong friendship,

build a strong trust. With time, relationships

prosper.

People want to have their cake and eat it too. Adults, when you are greedy, your

relationship can suffer a terrible emotional blow. Love your

job full time, love your family full time, pay yourself first.

Part-time your social life at your workplace. During

your time at work, minimize excessive conversation, and stay

focused on your mission to make your job a light load across the day or evening.

Exemplify overtime in your relationship.

When you put your relationship in front of your other responsibilities,

you will sustain a great relationship.

Pick Up the Pieces

There comes a time in life when we should pick up the pieces—for instance, when we break up in a relationship, when bad news comes all of a sudden, when we must pull ourselves together and move forward with our lives.

At times people feel great gaps or voids. If they become more spiritual or outgoing, chances are people will see that empty space go away swiftly.

Hobbies, goals, and objectives help us to pick up the pieces. If you are single and want a companion, send this message out into the universe, and eventually it will come to pass. Our lives can be compared to a puzzle. Everything happens for a reason at a time that sometimes seems unfair. To put the puzzle together, we must connect all events and learn from them, build, brainstorm, and move forward. Certainly, we must not get stuck in the past, but we can learn from past events and hopefully not make the same

decisions that put our life in delay, stress, or

aggravation mode.

Lastly, keep your pieces in perspective. Each piece is a

phase in life that you experience.

The Hourglass

Time, life, and opportunities are extremely valuable.

Thus when you are young, the hourglass that holds time should

not be taken for granted. The young

tend to think time will last forever.

We all know or should realize that we are not on this

planet for a long time, and we should be proactive, not

counteractive—or, as some would say, reactive. If you look

for trouble in the hood, make no mistake about it: you will get

it in the worst way. However, when you give someone bad-

attitude, indeed you will get it back.

People who do great things in life can have a prolonged

life. They learn

how to cope with stress and avoid stressful events.

Every minute, every second, every hour, and every day counts

inside the hourglass. Humble yourself in the hour of success,

smile every day, and be gracious toward everyone that helps you along the way. Moreover, give back to your community, and never

forget where you came from.

Never wait until the last minute, make every

second count, and live every day powerfully,

always taking charge of decisions that come your way

throughout life.

Delicious Diva

Let me tell you something: I love when a

woman knows how to dress, put on some smell-

good, and burn in the kitchen. Her skin is so pretty,

smooth, and irresistible. When a delicious diva

comes out into the public eye, heads turn,

and people say, "Wow, she's a hot commodity." Her body is so

sexy, her mind is right, and her approach is so tight. Hence

every brother appreciates a good sister.

A delicious diva's hair can be in a variety of

colors: red, brown, honey blonde, or jet black.

Regardless of the style, you can best believe

our ebony queens will step out of the house with

something that's out of sight.

Caution

You have to be more careful in the way you move

and who you hang around with. Learn to mind your business

and not pick trouble with people. The hood has your back

when you show love and respect. In retrospect, give back

to your community and keep our youth safe. The energy

that you send into the universe, for bad or good, will stick to you on
every level.

Tight face, screw face, I will punch you in the fast keeps

a lot of trouble, indeed double trouble that is impossible to get

out of. Needless to say, keep positive vibes.

Keep leadership and great opportunities in your life. Avoid the

yellow-tape lifestyle; go for a lifestyle of success, power,

and spiritual opportunity.

Count Down to Motivation

When you start at zero and you have nothing,

and you think success is always there, perhaps

it's in the form of positive energy through

powerful words, powerful circles, and most importantly,

travel and great exposure. You have to get

down, throw down, and bring down the house when

you are aiming to succeed in life.

1. We as individuals must love self first and

take care of self—that is, our health, wealth, spirituality, and family.

2. We must take steps in order to

succeed in our goals and objectives.

3. This is numbers one and two together:

think, dream, believe, and achieve, and

keep your plan of action in place to achieve all your goals

and objectives throughout life.

4. Every season you must pay yourself, take a vacation, and travel somewhere at least four times a year: winter,

spring, summer, and fall.

5. Do five powerful things daily to keep the motivation

in your heart. Push yourself, set goals, accomplish your

goals, believe in yourself, and most importantly, love yourself.

6. If you are in a meaningful relationship—meaning friends or marriage—these things can help: listen, learn,

do not judge, be patient, show love, and most importantly, stay

supportive.

7. When you have a job or career, these can also

help: presence, confidence, discipline, consistency,

constructive thinking, power thinking, and power moves.

No matter which way you count, always remember to count

your blessings, and never count yourself out of any great

opportunities.

Power for Our People of Color

Power for people of color has been here since the
beginning of time. People of color spend more money than any
race of people on the planet, so why can't we as a people stick
together, support each other, and utilize our money and effort for
our people. Yes, open Black-owned businesses empower our
youth with education, love, and support. Keep the
the power for the people of color movement active. Every home
must unite. Our culture as a whole must unite and not fight each
other, but love each other and fight for our right to succeed.

Be proud of our heritage, culture, and accomplishments.
Never make excuses for other cultures coming to the United States.
We have opportunities and must excel toward our blessings.
Keep your mind focused and your intensions straight
on course. Empower yourself with knowledge, finances, and love.
At every level, you must keep track of your success and
your goals so that you can measure where you need to be in each time
frame.

Being on time is right; staying consistent is right; staying ratchet-free is right;

and treating people with respect is definitely right.

Right or wrong, support people who do the right thing:

helping themselves, helping others, and using power thinking as the means

of success. By all means, we all are for our people in every culture.

Lastly, stay Black, bold, and beautiful, and keep the power for

our people of color on the top of your priority list every day.

Acknowledgments

My family was an inspiration for the creation of this book. My mother, grandmother, and aunt Joan—may they rest in peace—will forever be in my heart. Lydia Allen, Mardell Allen, and Joan Sharp were instrumental in teaching me the qualities of being a strong man, a great leader, and a great godparent of my two godchildren, Lamont and Lilly, who are being raised in a healthy, happy, powerful atmosphere. I would like to thank all of my family: the Allens and the Worthingtons, all over this country.

Printed in the United States
By Bookmasters

8/16